A Field Guide for Conducting Light Surveys of Outdoor Parking Lots

Edition One
June 2014

Kenneth R. Bryan
MPH (Industrial Hygiene)
University of South Florida

INTENTIONALLY BLANK

U.S. Copyright Applied for with the:

Library of Congress
Copyright Office
101 Independence Avenue, S.E.
Washington, D.C. 20559-6000

Reference Case #1-1483384991

INTENTIONALLY BLANK

Table of Contents

INTENTIONALLY BLANK

Introduction

This field guide has been developed to allow individuals, trained and experienced in the operation of a light meter, to conduct assessments of their exterior parking lot's lighting, as a component of more broadly based efforts to identify and abate risk to individuals and infrastructure which should include, but not be limited to, identification and characterization of risks, physical and operational security, as well as other measures.

Regrettably, there is significant debate amongst lighting professionals as to what constitutes adequate lighting in an outdoor parking lot and other outdoor areas. The Department of Homeland Security's interim Interagency Security Committee Standard 'Physical Security Criteria for Federal Facilities' dated April 12, 2010 permits open parking lots to be illuminated as low as 0.25 Foot Candles (fc).

Other professional literature, such as that developed by the very highly regarded Silva Consultants, indicates that for parking lot lighting an absolute minimum light level of 1 fc throughout the entire area is acceptable, and 2 to 4 fc being much more preferred.

This field guide is divided into four sections; the first describing the process for a comprehensive survey (the most reliable and accurate methodology), the second statistical sampling, and the third simplified sampling (the least reliable and accurate). The fourth section is devoted to the topic of calculated or theoretical illumination.

The users of this field guide are strongly encouraged to fully examine and utilize the wide array of mechanisms available to them as they explore and seek to understand the limitations of their outdoor parking lot lighting and forge ahead with solutions.

INTENTIONALLY BLANK

I. EXTERIOR PARKING LOT LIGHT SURVEY – COMPREHENSIVE SURVEY

Section One – Background Information

Date & Time of Evaluation: _____

Name of Evaluator: _____

Primary Telephone Number of Evaluator: _____

Business E-Mail Address of Evaluator:

_____

Survey Site: _____

Survey Site Address: _____

_____

Section Two – Environmental Conditions

Is the evaluation being conducted after sunset and before sunrise?

    Yes ⭕

    No ⭕

Cloud Conditions:

    Clear ⭕

    Not clear, but clouds cover less than ½ of sky ⭕

    Clouds cover more than ½ of sky, but not completely overcast ⭕

    Completely Overcast ⭕

Moon Phase:

Moon not visible ⭘

Visible, but less than or equal to ¼ of full ⭘

Visible, greater than ¼ of full but not more than ½ of full ⭘

Visible, more than ½ of full but not more than ¾ of full ⭘

Visible and more than ¾ full ⭘

Ongoing Precipitation (Rain, Snow, Sleet, Hail or Other):

Yes ⭘

No ⭘

Observed Lightening Flashes During Survey Period:

Yes ⭘

No ⭘

NOTE: PREFERRED CLOUD COVERAGE IS MORE THAN ½ (50%) OF SKY OR COMPLETELY OVERCAST. PREFERRED MOON PHASE IS LESS THAN ½ (50%) OF FULL. DURING THE SURVEY THERE SHOULD NOT BE ANY ONGOING PRECIPITATION OR ELECTRICAL STORM ACTIVITY.

Section Three – Light Measuring Instrumentation

Make and Model of Instrument: _____

_____

Is the outside temperature within the operating range of the instrument (if operating range of the instrument is unknown, presume that it is between 32°F and 104°F)?

Yes ◯

No ◯

Is the instrument being used by an individual trained in its use and in accordance with manufacturer's instructions?

Yes ◯

No ◯

Does the instrument appear to be functioning correctly?

Yes ◯

No ◯

Section Four – Existing Lighting

The outdoor parking lot is presently lighted by the following:

No electrical lighting	◯
Mercury Vapor lights	◯
Low Pressure Sodium	◯
High Pressure Sodium	◯
Metal Halide Lights	◯
LED Lighting	◯
Electrical lights of unknown type	◯

How many light bulbs are used to light the parking lot? (A light pole with ten clustered light bulbs would count as ten lights)

_____

Of the lights noted in the question above, how many are working?

_____

If there are any observable electrical hazards in the parking lot, please describe them below and immediately communicate the same to your supervisor and safety officer.

_____

_____

_____

Section Five – Conducting the Light Survey

Step One: Obtain a diagram of the parking lot, or draw an accurate representation of the parking lot in the below grid. Record the locations of existing lights and other significant features.

```
++++++++++++++++++++++++++++++++++++++++++++++++++++++++
++++++++++++++++++++++++++++++++++++++++++++++++++++++++
++++++++++++++++++++++++++++++++++++++++++++++++++++++++
++++++++++++++++++++++++++++++++++++++++++++++++++++++++
++++++++++++++++++++++++++++++++++++++++++++++++++++++++
++++++++++++++++++++++++++++++++++++++++++++++++++++++++
++++++++++++++++++++++++++++++++++++++++++++++++++++++++
++++++++++++++++++++++++++++++++++++++++++++++++++++++++
++++++++++++++++++++++++++++++++++++++++++++++++++++++++
++++++++++++++++++++++++++++++++++++++++++++++++++++++++
++++++++++++++++++++++++++++++++++++++++++++++++++++++++
++++++++++++++++++++++++++++++++++++++++++++++++++++++++
++++++++++++++++++++++++++++++++++++++++++++++++++++++++
++++++++++++++++++++++++++++++++++++++++++++++++++++++++
++++++++++++++++++++++++++++++++++++++++++++++++++++++++
++++++++++++++++++++++++++++++++++++++++++++++++++++++++
++++++++++++++++++++++++++++++++++++++++++++++++++++++++
++++++++++++++++++++++++++++++++++++++++++++++++++++++++
++++++++++++++++++++++++++++++++++++++++++++++++++++++++
++++++++++++++++++++++++++++++++++++++++++++++++++++++++
++++++++++++++++++++++++++++++++++++++++++++++++++++++++
++++++++++++++++++++++++++++++++++++++++++++++++++++++++
++++++++++++++++++++++++++++++++++++++++++++++++++++++++
++++++++++++++++++++++++++++++++++++++++++++++++++++++++
++++++++++++++++++++++++++++++++++++++++++++++++++++++++
++++++++++++++++++++++++++++++++++++++++++++++++++++++++
++++++++++++++++++++++++++++++++++++++++++++++++++++++++
++++++++++++++++++++++++++++++++++++++++++++++++++++++++
++++++++++++++++++++++++++++++++++++++++++++++++++++++++
++++++++++++++++++++++++++++++++++++++++++++++++++++++++
++++++++++++++++++++++++++++++++++++++++++++++++++++++++
```

Step Two: Begin the light survey at one end of the parking lot at the perimeter and holding the light meter in front of you so as to ensure that the light sensing mechanism isn't being blocked by your body take readings. Record them every twenty feet making sure that your diagram is annotated to properly reflect the site of the reading and its identifier, e.g. #1, #2 etcetera. Survey the entire parking lot in a grid fashion as indicated in the illustrated example of a 100 foot by 100 foot parking lot:

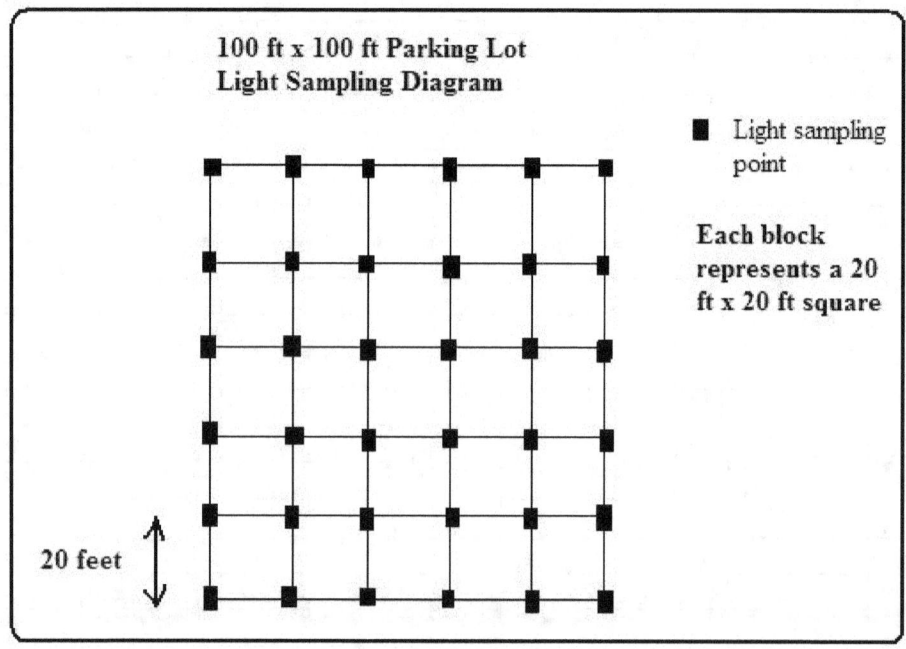

If the parking lot size is such that that when sampling is being conduct at twenty foot intervals that there is excess distance equal to or greater than 50% of the grid size, add additional sampling points. For example, if you had a 110 foot by 110 foot parking lot, you could reduce your grid size slightly and take seven samples per row (instead of six) and have seven rows (instead of six) for a total of forty-nine samples.

Readings in Foot Candles (One Foot Candle (fc) = 10.76 Lux)

Table 1.0 Light Meter Readings in Foot Candles (fc)

#1		#31		#61		#91	
#2		#32		#62		#92	
#3		#33		#63		#93	
#4		#34		#64		#94	
#5		#35		#65		#95	
#6		#36		#66		#96	
#7		#37		#67		#97	
#8		#38		#68		#98	
#9		#39		#69		#99	
#10		#40		#70		#100	
#11		#41		#71		#101	
#12		#42		#72		#102	
#13		#43		#73		#103	
#14		#44		#74		#104	
#15		#45		#75		#105	
#16		#46		#76		#106	
#17		#47		#77		#107	
#18		#48		#78		#108	
#19		#49		#79		#109	
#20		#50		#80		#110	
#21		#51		#81		#111	
#22		#52		#82		#112	
#23		#53		#83		#113	
#24		#54		#84		#114	
#25		#55		#85		#115	
#26		#56		#86		#116	
#27		#57		#87		#117	
#28		#58		#88		#118	
#29		#59		#89		#119	
#30		#60		#90		#120	

Section Six- Light Survey Analysis

Step One: Average Level of Parking Lot Lighting

Discussion: There is significant debate amongst lighting professionals as to what constitutes adequate lighting in an outdoor parking lot and other outdoor areas. The Department of Homeland Security's interim Interagency Security Committee Standard 'Physical Security Criteria for Federal Facilities' dated April 12, 2010 permits open parking lots to be illuminated as low as 0.25 Foot Candles (rounded from 0.23234). For covered parking areas under the same standard, required lighting is generally 1 Foot Candle, except for stairwells and lobbies where 2 Foot Candles is appropriate. Other professional literature, such as developed by the highly regard Silva Consultants, indicates that for parking lot lighting an absolute minimum light level of 1 fc throughout the entire area is acceptable and 2 to 4 fc being desired.

Add all of the Light level measurements recorded in Table 1.0 on page 15 together. Divide this number by the number of Light level measurements. This will result in your average outdoor parking lot light level in Foot Candles.

Line A - (Light level 1 + Light level 2 + Light level 3 ..... until last Light level measurement)

= _____

Line B - Number of total Light level readings = _____

Line C - Sum of all Light level measurements divided by number of total Light level readings to obtain the average level of parking lot lighting

(Line A divided by Line B) = _____

Results (Check one block)

Average parking lot lighting is less than 0.25 fc and
fails to meet the Department of Homeland Security's
interim Interagency Security Committee Standard   ◯
'Physical Security Criteria for Federal Facilities'
dated April 12, 2010.

Average parking lot lighting is equal to or greater
than 0.25 fc thus meeting the Department of
Homeland Security's interim Interagency Security   ◯
Committee Standard 'Physical Security Criteria
for Federal Facilities' dated April 12, 2010, however
does not meet the recommended absolute minimum
light level of 1 fc contained within some professional
literature.

Average parking lot lighting is equal to or greater
than 1.00 FC thus meeting the recommended absolute   ◯
minimum light level of 1 FC contained within some
professional literature but is less than optimal level of
at least 2 FC.

Average parking lot lighting is at least 2 FC.   ◯

Step Two: Uniformity Ratio

Discussion: The uniformity of lighting throughout an area is expressed in two ways; the ratio between the average lighting and the minimum lighting recorded, and the ratio between the maximum lighting recorded and the minimum lighting recorded. Uniformity of lighting is important because it takes time for individual's eyes to adjust, and during the period of adjustment increased risk may be created or lack of situational awareness could occur. There is significant debate amongst lighting professionals as to what constitutes the maximum uniformity rations in an outdoor parking lot and other outdoor areas which should exist. For the purpose of this lighting assessment, the Department of Homeland Security's interim Interagency Security Committee Standard 'Physical Security Criteria for Federal Facilities' dated April 12, 2010 guidance will be utilized.

Line A - The average level of parking lot lighting in fc as
      determined in Section Six, Step One (page 16)

      = _____

Line B - The minimum level of lighting in fc
      recorded within Table 1.0 (page 15)

      = _____

Line C - Line A divided by Line B = _____

NOTE: IF LINE A DIVIDED BY LINE B EXCEEDS 4.0, THEN THE UNIFORMITY RATIO IS TOO HIGH, AND CONSIDERATION SHOULD BE GIVEN TO TAKING APPROPRIATE MEASURES TO REDUCE THE RATIO.

Step Two: Uniformity Ratio (Continued)

Line D - The maximum level of lighting in fc
recorded within Table 1.0 (page 15) = _____

Line E - The minimum level of lighting in fc
recorded within Table 1.0 (page 15) = _____

Line F - Line D divided by Line E = _____

NOTE: IF LINE D DIVIDED BY LINE E EXCEEDS 20.0, THEN THE UNIFORMITY RATIO IS TOO HIGH, AND CONSIDERATION SHOULD BE GIVEN TO TAKING APPROPRIATE MEASURES TO REDUCE THE RATIO.

INTENTIONALLY BLANK

II. EXTERIOR PARKING LOT LIGHT SURVEY – STATISTICAL SAMPLING

Section One – Background Information

Date & Time of Evaluation: _____

Name of Evaluator: _____

Primary Telephone Number of Evaluator: _____

Business E-Mail Address of Evaluator:

_____

Survey Site: _____

Survey Site Address: _____

_____

Section Two – Environmental Conditions

Is the evaluation being conducted after sunset and before sunrise?

   Yes   ◯

   No   ◯

Cloud Conditions:

  Clear   ◯

  Not clear, but clouds cover less than ½ of sky   ◯

  Clouds cover more than ½ of sky, but not completely overcast ◯

  Completely Overcast   ◯

Moon Phase:

Moon not visible ○

Visible, but less than or equal to ¼ of full ○

Visible, greater than ¼ of full but not more than ½ of full ○

Visible, more than ½ of full but not more than ¾ of full ○

Visible and more than ¾ full ○

Ongoing Precipitation (Rain, Snow, Sleet, Hail or Other):

Yes ○

No ○

Observed Lightening Flashes During Survey Period:

Yes ○

No ○

NOTE: PREFERRED CLOUD COVERAGE IS MORE THAN ½ (50%) OF SKY OR COMPLETELY OVERCAST. PREFERRED MOON PHASE IS LESS THAN ½ (50%) OF FULL. DURING THE SURVEY THERE SHOULD NOT BE ANY ONGOING PRECIPITATION OR ELECTRICAL STORM ACTIVITY.

Section Three- Light Measuring Instrumentation

Make and Model of Instrument: _____

_____

Is the outside temperature within the operating range of the instrument (if operating range of the instrument is unknown, presume that it is between 32°F and 104°F)?

Yes ◯

No ◯

Is the instrument being used by an individual trained in its use and in accordance with manufacturer's instructions?

Yes ◯

No ◯

Does the instrument appear to be functioning correctly?

Yes ◯

No ◯

Section Four – Existing Lighting

The outdoor parking lot is presently lighted by the following:

No electrical lighting ○

Mercury Vapor lights ○

Low Pressure Sodium ○

High Pressure Sodium ○

Metal Halide Lights ○

LED Lighting ○

Electrical lights of unknown type ○

How many light bulbs are used to light the parking lot? (A light pole with ten clustered bulbs counts as ten lights)

_____

Of the light bulbs noted in the question above, how many are working?

_____

If there are any observable electrical hazards in the parking lot, please describe them below and immediately communicate the same to supervisor and/or safety officer.

_____

_____

Section Five – Conducting the Light Survey

Step One: Obtain a diagram of the parking lot, or draw an accurate representation of the parking lot in the below grid. Record the locations of existing lights and other significant features.

```
++++++++++++++++++++++++++++++++++++++++++++++++++++++++++++
++++++++++++++++++++++++++++++++++++++++++++++++++++++++++++
++++++++++++++++++++++++++++++++++++++++++++++++++++++++++++
++++++++++++++++++++++++++++++++++++++++++++++++++++++++++++
++++++++++++++++++++++++++++++++++++++++++++++++++++++++++++
++++++++++++++++++++++++++++++++++++++++++++++++++++++++++++
++++++++++++++++++++++++++++++++++++++++++++++++++++++++++++
++++++++++++++++++++++++++++++++++++++++++++++++++++++++++++
++++++++++++++++++++++++++++++++++++++++++++++++++++++++++++
++++++++++++++++++++++++++++++++++++++++++++++++++++++++++++
++++++++++++++++++++++++++++++++++++++++++++++++++++++++++++
++++++++++++++++++++++++++++++++++++++++++++++++++++++++++++
++++++++++++++++++++++++++++++++++++++++++++++++++++++++++++
++++++++++++++++++++++++++++++++++++++++++++++++++++++++++++
++++++++++++++++++++++++++++++++++++++++++++++++++++++++++++
++++++++++++++++++++++++++++++++++++++++++++++++++++++++++++
++++++++++++++++++++++++++++++++++++++++++++++++++++++++++++
++++++++++++++++++++++++++++++++++++++++++++++++++++++++++++
++++++++++++++++++++++++++++++++++++++++++++++++++++++++++++
++++++++++++++++++++++++++++++++++++++++++++++++++++++++++++
++++++++++++++++++++++++++++++++++++++++++++++++++++++++++++
++++++++++++++++++++++++++++++++++++++++++++++++++++++++++++
++++++++++++++++++++++++++++++++++++++++++++++++++++++++++++
++++++++++++++++++++++++++++++++++++++++++++++++++++++++++++
++++++++++++++++++++++++++++++++++++++++++++++++++++++++++++
++++++++++++++++++++++++++++++++++++++++++++++++++++++++++++
++++++++++++++++++++++++++++++++++++++++++++++++++++++++++++
++++++++++++++++++++++++++++++++++++++++++++++++++++++++++++
++++++++++++++++++++++++++++++++++++++++++++++++++++++++++++
++++++++++++++++++++++++++++++++++++++++++++++++++++++++++++
++++++++++++++++++++++++++++++++++++++++++++++++++++++++++++
++++++++++++++++++++++++++++++++++++++++++++++++++++++++++++
```

Discussion: Statistical sampling permits the expenditure of less time, energy and labor to assess the adequacy of outdoor parking lot lighting (particularly very large ones) through the elimination of the need to measure every single point within the parking lot matrix drawn in Section Five provided that the sampling strategy is representative, and a statistically valid sample of the whole is taken. It has the disadvantage of having a lower probability or confidence level. The statistical sampling method used for this assessment will have a confidence level of 95%; Margin of error + or – 5%.

The use of statistical sampling is only recommended for very large outdoor parking lots which would require more than 150 light meter readings.

Table 1.0 Table for Determining Random Sample Size from a Given Population

(Confidence level 95%; Margin of Error + or minus 5%)

Population N	Sample S	Population N	Sample S	Population N	Sample S
10	10	100	80	280	162
15	14	110	86	290	165
20	19	120	82	300	169
25	24	130	97	320	175
30	28	140	103	340	181
35	32	150	108	360	186
40	36	160	113	380	191
45	40	170	118	400	196
50	44	180	123	420	201
55	48	190	127	440	205
60	52	200	132	460	210
65	56	210	136	480	214
70	59	220	140	500	217
75	63	230	144	550	226
80	66	240	148	600	234
85	70	250	152	650	242
90	73	260	155	700	248
95	76	270	159	750	254

Source: Payne, D.A. and Morris, R. F. (1967). Educational and Psychological Measurement. Waltham, Mass., Blaisdell Pub. Co.

Step Two: Determination of Population Size

Utilizing the drawing made in Section Five Step One, determine the maximum number of light meter readings which would have been made had a full light survey been conducted. Don't forget to include the perimeter readings which would have been performed using a 20 foot x 20 foot grid. If the parking lot size is such that that when sampling is being conduct at twenty foot intervals that there is excess distance equal to or greater than 50% of the grid size, add additional sampling points. For example, if you had a 110 foot by 110 foot parking lot, you could reduce your grid size slightly and take seven samples per row (instead of six) and have seven rows (instead of six) for a total of forty-nine samples.

Number of light meter readings based on parking lot size using the comprehensive survey criteria

= _____

Utilizing Table 2.0 determine the number of light meter readings based on statistical sampling (Confidence level 95%; Margin of Error plus or minus 5%)

= _____

Using your new sample size for the statistical sample and your drawing establish a sample grid. Distances throughout the grid should be proximately equivalent to each other and will be larger than the 20 foot x 20 foot grid established using the comprehensive survey criteria.

Step Three: Taking Light Meter Readings

Begin the light survey at one end of the parking lot at the perimeter and holding the light meter in front of you so as to ensure that the light sensing mechanism isn't being blocked by your body take readings. Record them making sure that your diagram is annotated to properly reflect the site of the reading and its identifier, e.g. #1, #2 etcetera. Survey the entire parking lot in a grid fashion.

Readings in Foot Candles (One Foot Candle (fc) = 10.76 Lux)

Table 1.0 Light Meter Readings in Foot Candles (fc)

#		#		#		#	
#1		#31		#61		#91	
#2		#32		#62		#92	
#3		#33		#63		#93	
#4		#34		#64		#94	
#5		#35		#65		#95	
#6		#36		#66		#96	
#7		#37		#67		#97	
#8		#38		#68		#98	
#9		#39		#69		#99	
#10		#40		#70		#100	
#11		#41		#71		#101	
#12		#42		#72		#102	
#13		#43		#73		#103	
#14		#44		#74		#104	
#15		#45		#75		#105	
#16		#46		#76		#106	
#17		#47		#77		#107	
#18		#48		#78		#108	
#19		#49		#79		#109	
#20		#50		#80		#110	
#21		#51		#81		#111	
#22		#52		#82		#112	
#23		#53		#83		#113	
#24		#54		#84		#114	
#25		#55		#85		#115	
#26		#56		#86		#116	
#27		#57		#87		#117	
#28		#58		#88		#118	
#29		#59		#89		#119	
#30		#60		#90		#120	

Section Six – Light Survey Analysis

Step One: Calculate the Standard Deviation for the Population

Discussion: For larger populations, where N ≥ 30, we will consider σ and s to be proximate equivalents, as well as μ and x-bar.

$$\sigma = \sqrt{\frac{1}{N}\sum_{i=1}^{N}(x_i - \mu)^2}$$

Where: Standard Deviation is σ
the mean of the values is μ
the individual x values are x_i
number of samples is N for N ≥ 30

Find the mean. The mean is the average of all your samples. Add each sample number and then divide by the number of samples.

The mean of the sample (μ) = _____

Then find the variance. The variance is the average of the squared differences from the mean. To get the variance, first calculate the difference from the mean for each sample number. Square each number then average the results.

The standard deviation is the square root of the variance. This number will tell you how closely your samples are located to the mean. Usually, approximately 68% of all the samples will fall inside one standard deviation from the mean.

Standard Deviation (σ) = _____

Step Two: Initiate One Tailed (Lower Tailed) Hypothesis Test with level α 0.05 for parking lot lighting meeting or exceeding Physical Security Criteria for Federal Facilities Interagency Security Committee Standard dated April 12, 2010 of 0.25 foot candle (fc) lighting level.

Null and Alternative Hypotheses

$H_0 = \mu \geq 0.25$
H_0 = the mean of the sample light readings is greater than or equal to 0.25 fc

$H_1 = \mu < 0.25$
H_1 = the mean of the sample light readings is less than 0.25 fc

Calculation of Test Statistic

$Z = \overline{(x} - \mu_0) \div (\sigma/\sqrt{n})$
Z = (mean of sample measured in fc – 0.25 fc) divided by (standard deviation divided by the square root of the number of samples)

Note: For larger populations, where N ≥ 30, we will consider σ and s to be proximate equivalents, as well as μ and x-bar.

If the Z value is smaller than negative 1.645 (e.g. -1.7, -1.8, -1.9 etc) then the test statistic is in the rejection region. Therefore we can reject the null hypothesis in favor of the alternative. Thus we can conclude that the mean lighting level is significantly less than the 0.25 fc required under the Federal Facilities Interagency Security Committee Standard dated April 12, 2010.

If the Z value is equal to or greater than negative 1.645 (e.g. -1.6, -1.5, -1.4 etc) then we cannot reject the null hypothesis.

Step Three: Initiate One Tailed (Lower Tailed) Hypothesis Test with level α 0.05 for parking lot lighting meeting or exceeding of 1.0 foot candle (fc) lighting level.

Null and Alternative Hypotheses

$H_0 = \mu \geq 1.0$
$H_0 =$ the mean of the sample light readings is greater than or equal to 1.0 fc

$H_1 = \mu < 1.0$
$H_1 =$ the mean of the sample light readings is less than 1.0 fc

Calculation of Test Statistic

$Z = \overline{(x} - \mu_0) \div (\sigma/\sqrt{n})$
$Z =$ (mean of sample measured in fc – 1.0 fc) divided by (standard deviation divided by the square root of the number of samples)

Note: For larger populations, where $N \geq 30$, we will consider σ and s to be proximate equivalents, as well as μ and x-bar.

If the Z value is smaller than negative 1.645 (e.g. – 1.7, - 1.8, - 1.9 etc) then the test statistic is in the rejection region. Therefore we can reject the null hypothesis in favor of the alternative. Thus we can conclude that the mean lighting level is significantly less than the 1.0 fc recommended as being the absolute minimal lighting level by many private consultants.

If the Z value is equal to or greater than negative 1.645 (e.g. -1.6, -1.5, -1.4 etc) then we cannot reject the null hypothesis.

Step Four: Initiate One Tailed (Lower Tailed) Hypothesis Test with level α 0.05 for parking lot lighting meeting or exceeding of 2.0 foot candle (fc) lighting level.

Null and Alternative Hypotheses

$H_0 = \mu \geq 2.0$
H_0 = the mean of the sample light readings is
   greater than or equal to 2.0 fc

$H_1 = \mu < 1.0$
H_1 = the mean of the sample light readings is less than 2.0 fc

Calculation of Test Statistic

$Z = \overline{(x - \mu_0)} \div (\sigma/\sqrt{n})$
Z = (mean of sample measured in fc – 2.0 fc) divided by
   (standard deviation divided by the square root
   of the number of samples)

Note: For larger populations, where $N \geq 30$, we will consider σ and s to be proximate equivalents, as well as μ and x-bar.

If the Z value is smaller than negative 1.645 (e.g. – 1.7, - 1.8, - 1.9 etc) then the test statistic is in the rejection region. Therefore we can reject the null hypothesis in favor of the alternative. Thus we can conclude that the mean lighting level is significantly less than the 2.0 fc recommended as being the optimal minimal lighting level by many private consultants.

If the Z value is equal to or greater than negative 1.645 (e.g. -1.6, -1.5, -1.4 etc) then we cannot reject the null hypothesis.

Step Five: Uniformity Ratio

Discussion: The uniformity of lighting throughout an area is expressed in two ways; the ratio between the average lighting and the minimum lighting recorded, and the ratio between the maximum lighting recorded and the minimum lighting recorded. Uniformity of lighting is important because it takes time for individual's eyes to adjust, and during the period of adjustment increased risk may be created or lack of situational awareness could occur. There is significant debate amongst lighting professionals as to what constitutes the maximum uniformity rations in an outdoor parking lot and other outdoor areas which should exist. For the purpose of this lighting assessment, the Department of Homeland Security's interim Interagency Security Committee Standard 'Physical Security Criteria for Federal Facilities' dated April 12, 2010 guidance will be utilized.

Line A - The average level of parking lot lighting in fc
as determined in Section Six, Step One (page 30)

= _____

Line B - The minimum level of lighting in fc
recorded within Table 1.0 (page 29)

= _____

Line C - Line A divided by Line B = _____

NOTE: IF LINE A DIVIDED BY LINE B EXCEEDS 4.0, THEN THE UNIFORMITY RATIO IS TOO HIGH, AND CONSIDERATION SHOULD BE GIVEN TO TAKING APPROPRIATE MEASURES TO REDUCE THE RATIO.

Step Five: Uniformity Ratio (Continued)

Line D - The maximum level of lighting in fc
      recorded within Table 1.0 (page 29) = _____

Line E - The minimum level of lighting in fc
      recorded within Table 1.0 (page 29) = _____

Line F- Line D divided by Line E = _____

NOTE: IF LINE D DIVIDED BY LINE E EXCEEDS 20.0, THEN THE UNIFORMITY RATIO IS TOO HIGH, AND CONSIDERATION SHOULD BE GIVEN TO TAKING APPROPRIATE MEASURES TO REDUCE THE RATIO.

III. EXTERIOR PARKING LOT LIGHT SURVEY – SIMPLIFIED SAMPLING

Section One – Background Information

Date & Time of Evaluation: _____

Name of Evaluator:_____

Primary Telephone Number of Evaluator: _____

Business E-Mail Address of Evaluator:

_____

Survey Site: _____

Survey Site Address: _____

_____

Section Two – Environmental Conditions

Is the evaluation being conducted after sunset and before sunrise?

    Yes   ◯

    No   ◯

Cloud Conditions:

    Clear   ◯

    Not clear, but clouds cover less than ½ of sky   ◯

    Clouds cover more than ½ of sky, but not completely overcast   ◯

    Completely Overcast   ◯

Moon Phase:

Moon not visible ○

Visible, but less than or equal to ¼ of full ○

Visible, greater than ¼ of full but not more than ½ of full ○

Visible, more than ½ of full but not more than ¾ of full ○

Visible and more than ¾ full ○

Ongoing Precipitation (Rain, Snow, Sleet, Hail or Other):

Yes ○

No ○

Observed Lightening Flashes During Survey Period:

Yes ○

No ○

NOTE: PREFERRED CLOUD COVERAGE IS MORE THAN ½ (50%) OF SKY OR COMPLETELY OVERCAST. PREFERRED MOON PHASE IS LESS THAN ½ (50%) OF FULL. DURING THE SURVEY THERE SHOULD NOT BE ANY ONGOING PRECIPITATION OR ELECTRICAL STORM ACTIVITY.

Section Three – Light Measuring Instrumentation

Make and Model of Instrument: _____

_____

Is the outside temperature within the operating range of the instrument (if operating range of the instrument is unknown, presume that it is between 32°F and 104°F)?

Yes ○

No ○

Is the instrument being used by an individual trained in its use and in accordance with manufacturer's instructions?

Yes ○

No ○

Does the instrument appear to be functioning correctly?

Yes ○

No ○

Section Four – Existing Lighting

The outdoor parking lot is presently lighted by the following:

No electrical lighting   ◯

Mercury Vapor lights   ◯

Low Pressure Sodium   ◯

High Pressure Sodium   ◯

Metal Halide Lights   ◯

LED Lighting   ◯

Electrical lights of unknown type   ◯

How many light bulbs are used to light the parking lot? (A light pole with ten clustered bulbs would count as ten lights)

_____

Of the light bulbs noted in the question above, how many are working?

_____

If there are any observable electrical hazards in the parking lot, please describe them below and immediately communicate the same to your supervisor and safety officer.

_____

_____

Section Five – Conducting the Light Survey

Step One: Obtain a diagram of the parking lot, or draw an accurate representation of the parking lot in the below grid. Record the locations of existing lights and other significant features.

```
++++++++++++++++++++++++++++++++++++++++++++++++++++++++++++
++++++++++++++++++++++++++++++++++++++++++++++++++++++++++++
++++++++++++++++++++++++++++++++++++++++++++++++++++++++++++
++++++++++++++++++++++++++++++++++++++++++++++++++++++++++++
++++++++++++++++++++++++++++++++++++++++++++++++++++++++++++
++++++++++++++++++++++++++++++++++++++++++++++++++++++++++++
++++++++++++++++++++++++++++++++++++++++++++++++++++++++++++
++++++++++++++++++++++++++++++++++++++++++++++++++++++++++++
++++++++++++++++++++++++++++++++++++++++++++++++++++++++++++
++++++++++++++++++++++++++++++++++++++++++++++++++++++++++++
++++++++++++++++++++++++++++++++++++++++++++++++++++++++++++
++++++++++++++++++++++++++++++++++++++++++++++++++++++++++++
++++++++++++++++++++++++++++++++++++++++++++++++++++++++++++
++++++++++++++++++++++++++++++++++++++++++++++++++++++++++++
++++++++++++++++++++++++++++++++++++++++++++++++++++++++++++
++++++++++++++++++++++++++++++++++++++++++++++++++++++++++++
++++++++++++++++++++++++++++++++++++++++++++++++++++++++++++
++++++++++++++++++++++++++++++++++++++++++++++++++++++++++++
++++++++++++++++++++++++++++++++++++++++++++++++++++++++++++
++++++++++++++++++++++++++++++++++++++++++++++++++++++++++++
++++++++++++++++++++++++++++++++++++++++++++++++++++++++++++
++++++++++++++++++++++++++++++++++++++++++++++++++++++++++++
++++++++++++++++++++++++++++++++++++++++++++++++++++++++++++
++++++++++++++++++++++++++++++++++++++++++++++++++++++++++++
++++++++++++++++++++++++++++++++++++++++++++++++++++++++++++
++++++++++++++++++++++++++++++++++++++++++++++++++++++++++++
++++++++++++++++++++++++++++++++++++++++++++++++++++++++++++
++++++++++++++++++++++++++++++++++++++++++++++++++++++++++++
++++++++++++++++++++++++++++++++++++++++++++++++++++++++++++
++++++++++++++++++++++++++++++++++++++++++++++++++++++++++++
```

Step Two: Begin the light survey at one end of the parking lot at the perimeter and holding the light meter in front of you so as to ensure that the light sensing mechanism isn't being blocked by your body take readings. Record them every fifty feet making sure that your diagram is annotated to properly reflect the site of the reading and its identifier, e.g. #1, #2 etcetera. Survey the entire parking lot in a grid fashion as indicated in the illustrated example of a 250 foot by 250 foot parking lot:

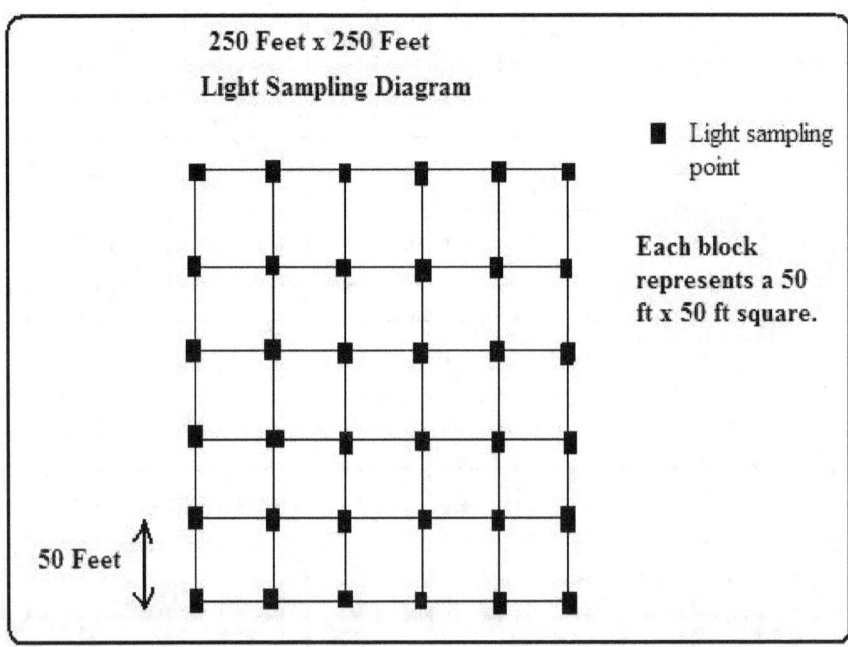

If the parking lot size is such that that when sampling is being conduct at twenty foot intervals that there is excess distance equal to or greater than 50% of the grid size, add additional sampling points. For example, if you had a 280 foot by 280 foot parking lot, you could reduce your grid size slightly and take seven samples per row (instead of six) and have seven rows (instead of six) for a total of forty-nine samples.

Readings in Foot Candles (One Foot Candle (fc) = 10.76 Lux)

Table 1.0 Light Meter Readings in Foot Candles (fc)

#1		#31		#61		#91	
#2		#32		#62		#92	
#3		#33		#63		#93	
#4		#34		#64		#94	
#5		#35		#65		#95	
#6		#36		#66		#96	
#7		#37		#67		#97	
#8		#38		#68		#98	
#9		#39		#69		#99	
#10		#40		#70		#100	
#11		#41		#71		#101	
#12		#42		#72		#102	
#13		#43		#73		#103	
#14		#44		#74		#104	
#15		#45		#75		#105	
#16		#46		#76		#106	
#17		#47		#77		#107	
#18		#48		#78		#108	
#19		#49		#79		#109	
#20		#50		#80		#110	
#21		#51		#81		#111	
#22		#52		#82		#112	
#23		#53		#83		#113	
#24		#54		#84		#114	
#25		#55		#85		#115	
#26		#56		#86		#116	
#27		#57		#87		#117	
#28		#58		#88		#118	
#29		#59		#89		#119	
#30		#60		#90		#120	

Section Six- Light Survey Analysis

Step One: Average Level of Parking Lot Lighting

Discussion: There is significant debate amongst lighting professionals as to what constitutes adequate lighting in an outdoor parking lot and other outdoor areas. The Department of Homeland Security's interim Interagency Security Committee Standard 'Physical Security Criteria for Federal Facilities' dated April 12, 2010 permits open parking lots to be illuminated as low as 0.25 Foot Candles (fc). Other professional literature, such as that developed by the very highly regarded Silva Consultants, indicates that for parking lot lighting an absolute minimum light level of 1 fc throughout the entire area is acceptable, and 2 to 4 fc being desired.

Insomuch that this simplified sampling regimen results in approximately 75% less sampling than the comprehensive survey, minimum recorded light levels have been raised to account for the increased margin of error and greater variation.

Add all of the Light level measurements recorded in Table 1.0 on page 6 together. Divide this number by the number of Light level measurements. This will result in your average outdoor parking lot light level in Foot Candles.

Line A - (Light level 1 + Light level 2 + Light level 3 ….. until last
Light level measurement)

= _____

Line B - Number of total Light level readings = _____

Line C - Sum of all Light level measurements divided by number of
total Light level readings to obtain the average level of
parking lot lighting

(Line A divided by Line B) = _____

Results (Check one block)

The simplified sampling average parking lot lighting
is less than 0.50 fc and may not meet the Department
of Homeland Security's interim Interagency Security
Committee Standard 'Physical Security Criteria for
Federal Facilities' dated April 12, 2010. A comprehensive
survey or statistical sampling is recommended.
○

The simplified sampling average parking lot lighting is
equal to or greater than 0.50 fc, thus most likely meeting
the Department of Homeland Security's interim Interagency
Security Committee Standard 'Physical Security Criteria
for Federal Facilities' dated April 12, 2010, however may
not meet the recommended absolute minimum light level of
2 fc (1 fc comprehensive survey level with correction factor
to account for simplified sampling contained within some
professional literature. A comprehensive survey or statistical
sampling is recommended.
○

The simplified sampling average parking lot lighting is
equal to or greater than 2.00 fc thus most likely meets
the recommended absolute minimum light level of 1 fc
contained within some professional literature but is less
than optimal level of at least 4 fc (2 fc comprehensive
survey level with correction factor to account for simplified
sampling).
○

Average parking lot lighting is at least 4 fc (2 fc
comprehensive survey level with correction factor
to account for simplified sampling).
○

Step Two: Uniformity Ratio

Discussion: The uniformity of lighting throughout an area is expressed in two ways; the ratio between the average lighting and the minimum lighting recorded, and the ratio between the maximum lighting recorded and the minimum lighting recorded. Uniformity of lighting is important because it takes time for individual's eyes to adjust, and during the period of adjustment increased risk may be created or lack of situational awareness could occur. There is significant debate amongst lighting professionals as to what constitutes the maximum uniformity rations in an outdoor parking lot and other outdoor areas which should exist. For the purpose of this lighting assessment, the Department of Homeland Security's interim Interagency Security Committee Standard 'Physical Security Criteria for Federal Facilities' dated April 12, 2010 guidance will be utilized.

Line A - The average level of parking lot lighting in fc
as determined in Section Six, Step One (page 43)

= _____

Line B - The minimum level of lighting in fc
recorded within Table 1.0 (page 42)

= _____

Line C - Line A divided by Line B = _____

NOTE: IF LINE A DIVIDED BY LINE B EXCEEDS 4.0, THEN THE UNIFORMITY RATIO IS TOO HIGH, AND CONSIDERATION SHOULD BE GIVEN TO TAKING APPROPRIATE MEASURES TO REDUCE THE RATIO.

Line D - The maximum level of lighting in fc
       recorded within Table 1.0 (page 42)

       = _____

Line E - The minimum level of lighting in fc
       recorded within Table 1.0 (page 42)

       = _____

Line F - Line D divided by Line E = _____

NOTE: IF LINE D DIVIDED BY LINE E EXCEEDS 20.0, THEN THE UNIFORMITY RATIO IS TOO HIGH, AND CONSIDERATION SHOULD BE GIVEN TO TAKING APPROPRIATE MEASURES TO REDUCE THE RATIO.

IV. CALCULATED OR THEORETICAL ILLUMINATION

The calculated or theoretical illumination for an area can be mathematically determined using the following standard formula:

$$E = [(n \times N \times F \times UF \times LLF) \div A]$$

where E = the average illuminance over the horizontal working plane

n = the number of lamps in each luminaire

N = the number of luminaire

F = the lighting design lumens per lamp, i.e. initial bare lamp luminous flux

UF = utilization factor for the horizontal working plane

LLF = light loss factor.

A = area of the horizontal working plane

The light loss factor is itself a product of the lamp lumen maintenance factor multiplied (LLMF) by the luminaire maintenance factor (LMF) multiplied by the room surface maintenance factor (RSMF).

While the calculated or theoretical illumination method is useful in the initial outdoor parking lot design and for potentially correcting lighting deficiencies in a poorly lit lot, reliance on calculated or theoretical illumination as a substitute for actual observed light conditions is not recommended.

Glossary

Foot Candle (fc) - *A unit of measure of the intensity of light falling on a surface, equal to one lumen per square foot and originally defined with reference to a standardized candle burning at one foot from a given surface.*

Light Loss Factor (LLF) - *The ratio of the illuminance produced by the lighting installation at the some specified time to the illuminance produced by the same installation when new.*

Lamp Lumen Maintenance Factor (LLMF) - *is the proportion of the initial light output of a lamp produced after a set time to those produced when new.*

Light Meter - *An electronic instrument, generally portable, which reliably and accurately measures illumination and provides an indication of the level of illumination in the form of a visual display.*

Light Survey - *An audit of natural and artificial illumination conducted in a defined area by a trained individual utilizing instrumentation which quantifies light levels, generally in foot candles and/or lumens, thus allowing an assessment of the adequacy of the illumination.*

Outdoor Parking Lot - *A dedicated, usually uncovered off-street area where motor vehicles are stored outside for short periods in a location that allow drivers and passengers access to employment, businesses, recreation, housing and other transportation. Frequently parking is on a durable or semi-durable surface such as concrete, macadam, brick, stone, or tire-tread woven mats. Outdoor parking lots are frequently lit with artificial lighting generally located on poles. A parking garage, even the upper most level which is nearly always uncovered, is not considered to be an outdoor parking lot.*

Statistical Sampling - *The process of selecting elements of a population for either descriptive or inferential purposes in a manner which allows for conclusions to be made about the total population from the selected elements, within a given confidence level and allowance for sampling risk.*

Notes/Calculations/Misc.

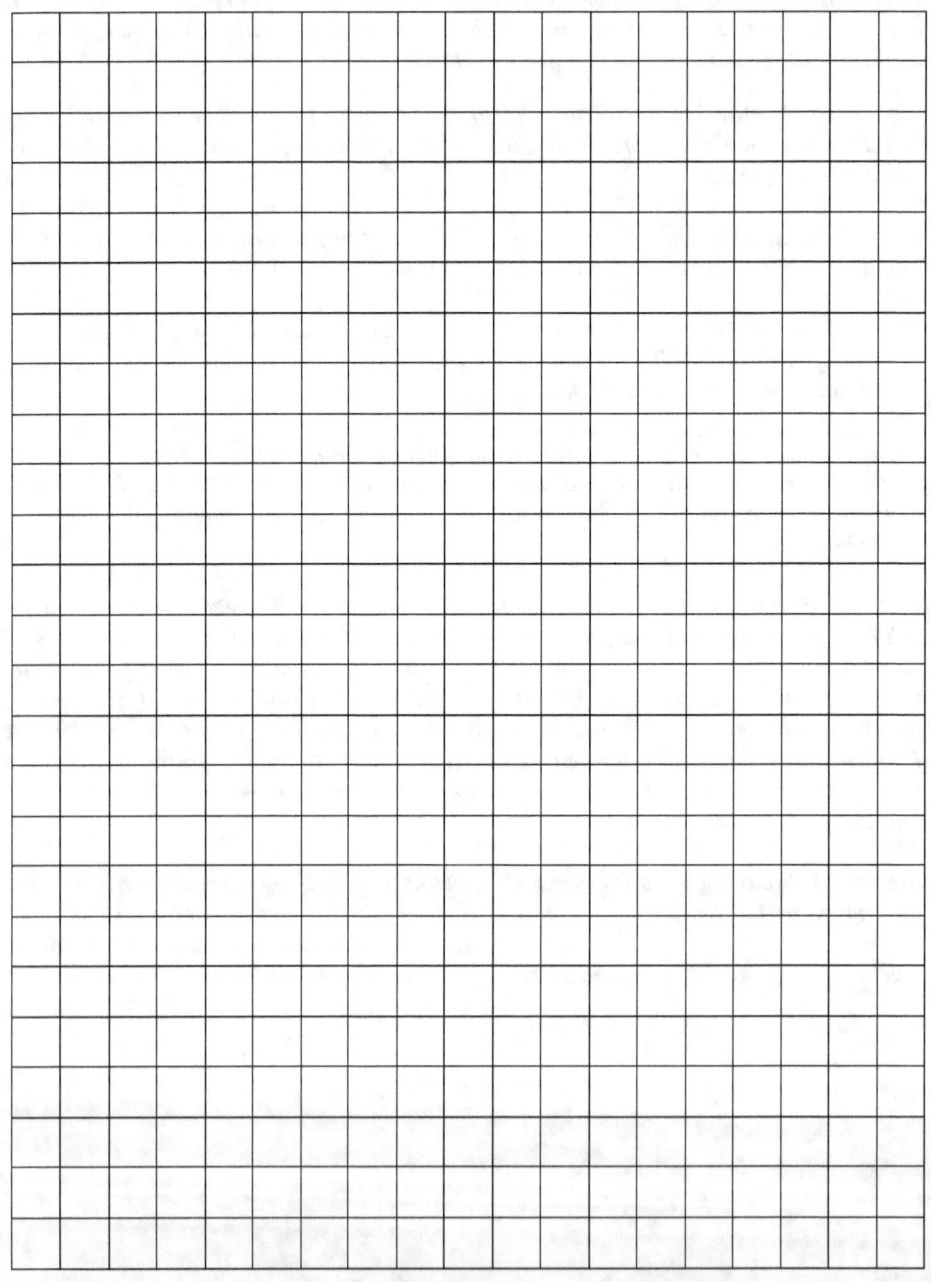

Notes/Calculations/Misc.

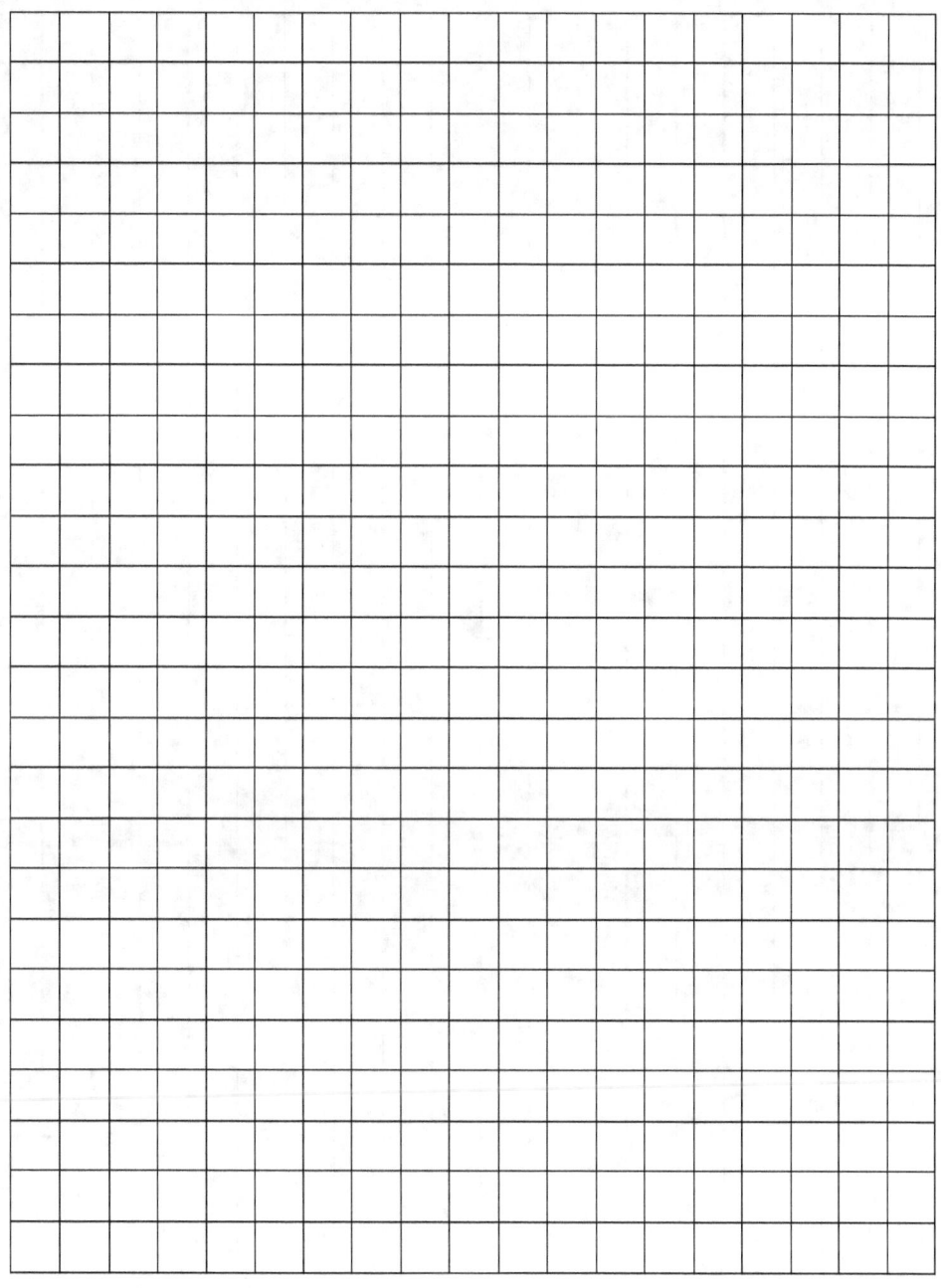

Notes/Calculations/Misc.

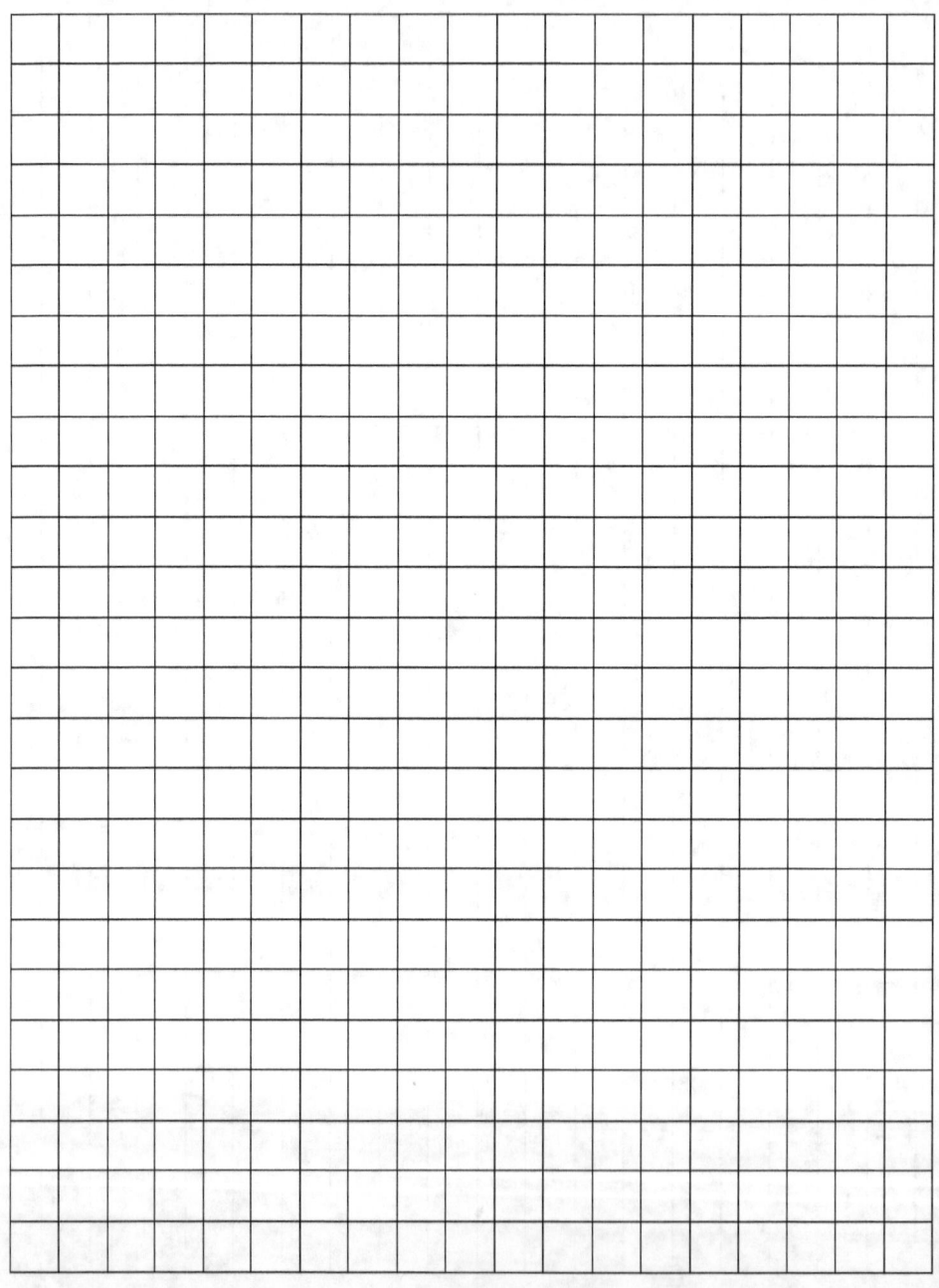